Exemplary Science:
Best Practices in
Professional Development